THE
WEIGHTY WORD
BOOK

Copyright © 1985,
Paul M. Levitt, Douglas A. Burger, and Elissa S. Guralnick

Illustrations by Janet Stevens

Library of Congress Card Catalog Number 85-062731
ISBN 0-917665-13-9

Published in 1985 in the United States of America by
BOOKMAKERS GUILD, INC.
1430 Florida Avenue, Suite 202
Longmont, Colorado 80501
in cooperation with the University of Colorado Foundation
PO Box 1140
Boulder, Colorado 80306

Second printing 1986, by Bookmakers Guild, Inc.

Printed and bound in the United States of America

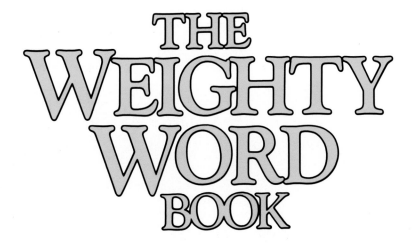

Paul M. Levitt

Douglas A. Burger

Elissa S. Guralnick

with illustrations by

Janet Stevens

Published by Bookmakers Guild, Inc., Longmont, Colorado
in cooperation with the University of Colorado Foundation

For

the Levitt lads and lass

Scot, Daniel, and Andrea

the Burger boys

Steven and Daniel

the Guralnick gang

Joanna and Daniel

Acknowledgment

We are deeply grateful to the University of
Colorado Foundation and, in particular, to
Charlie McCord and Gene Wilson.

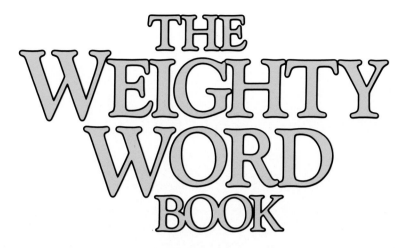

THE WEIGHTY WORD BOOK

CONTENTS
AND COLOR ILLUSTRATIONS

Introduction

If a picture is worth a thousand words, one big word, correctly used, is worth numerous little words. The big words in this book—one for each letter of the alphabet—have been selected not only for their frequency in the written language, but also for their sound. In every instance, the word has more than one syllable and the sound of the word lends itself to a pun.

The stories in the book are, as you will see, suggested by the pun. Although the stories are fanciful, they lead to the correct meaning of the words. By recalling the story and the concluding pun, children ought to remember the meaning of the word. The stories and the puns, therefore, serve as memory hooks and encourage children to increase their vocabulary by forming their own mnemonics for any new words they encounter.

P.M.L.
D.A.B.
E.S.G.

Benjamin Van Der Bellows worked for a very large and busy steamship company, with offices all over the world. Benjamin's office was in New York and commanded a view of the New York skyline, from the Hudson River to the East River, and from the Bronx to the Village. Located at the top of the Cloudhigh Building, Benjamin's office was on the 40th floor.

Benjamin was proud of his office. "You're a lucky man, Bellows," a customer would remark; and Benjamin would reply, "The largest offices and the best secretaries are, of course, reserved for the most important people." Then he would cough and turn to one of his secretaries and say something like, "Take this down, Miss Rightwell. The next steamship from Oslo will stop at Plymouth on the way to Rotterdam." And Miss Rightwell would interrupt and say something like, "I beg your pardon, Mr. Van Der Bellows, but the next steamship from Oslo will *not* stop at Plymouth on the way to Rotterdam." Benjamin, you see, simply did not know the things he was supposed to know. He was, in fact, not very smart.

1

The President of the steamship company finally decided that because of his many mistakes, Benjamin would have to step down. He called Benjamin to his office and said, "Bellows, I am moving you from the 40th floor to the 20th." Benjamin couldn't believe his ears. Nevertheless, he moved down to the 20th floor, where his new office was half as large as his old. Here he had a view of 20th Street, with all its stalls and open markets. When customers came to call on him, he would lean back in his chair, survey his office, and say, "This office, of course, is only temporary. I will be moving upstairs in a few weeks."

But in fact he did not move upstairs. Called into the President's office a few months later, Benjamin said, "If you'd like me to take my old quarters on the 40th floor, I can be packed and ready to move upstairs in a couple of hours." The President shuffled some papers on his desk and replied, "As a matter of fact, Bellows, I had in mind another direction—downstairs, to the 10th floor." Benjamin was amazed. "Downstairs, to the 10th floor," he said, "whatever for?" The President drew a piece of paper out of the pile in front of him and said, "Remember, Bellows, that load of cargo you ordered shipped up the Nile to Cairo, Egypt?" "Yes," answered Benjamin. "Well," said the President, "it was supposed to be shipped up the Mississippi to Cairo, Illinois!"

The next day, Benjamin moved into his new office on the 10th floor. Although this office was only half as large as the one on the 20th floor, it had a good view of 10th Avenue and the docks. But only a few weeks later, Benjamin was called to the President's office. "Bellows," said the President, "you're moving downstairs." Benjamin was crushed. "There must be some mistake," he said. "Yes," the President replied, "dozens! Remember the bathing suits that went to Iceland and the fur coats that went to the Sahara!" Benjamin wiped his brow and replied, "Well, nobody's perfect." The President angrily responded, "That's for sure!"

Then the President leaned back in his chair and said, "Bellows, water seeks its own level, and so does ability. You're fit for an office in a basement!"

So, whenever a person has been lowered in position or rank or office, just as Benjamin was lowered from a 40th floor office to a basement, we say that person has suffered

Josephine and Kate were identical twins. They not only looked and dressed alike, they also behaved alike. Whatever one did, the other did. If Josephine rode with "no hands" on her bicycle, Kate did also; if Kate water-skied on one ski, Josephine did also. At school, it was the same way: if Josephine studied French, Kate did also; if Kate joined the Theatre Club, Josephine did also.

When they were grown, they lived in the same house and worked at the same travel agency. They even took their vacations at the same time. Together they climbed mountains in Switzerland, sailed iceboats in Norway, and collected coral from the waters of Sicily. But one year, the most amazing thing happened: Josephine wanted to do one thing, and Kate another! Josephine wanted to visit Iceland, and Kate wanted to visit Luxembourg.

"Luxembourg!" Josephine exclaimed. "It's so small! In one day, we'll run out of sights to see. But in Iceland we'll be able to see fiords and waterfalls and geysers and fishing villages. What does Luxembourg have?"

"Luxembourg, my dear sister Josephine," said Kate, "has deep winding valley streams and forests of oak and birch and beech. In all of Iceland I don't think there's a single tree!" "Iceland," said Josephine triumphantly, "has volcanoes!" "Luxembourg," answered Kate, "has a Grand Palace and a Town Hall and a famous Cathedral!" "Iceland," snorted Josephine, "has chess tournaments!" "So what?" answered Kate; "you don't even know how to play chess!" "I can watch," answered Josephine. "Then watch by yourself," said Kate, "because I am going to Luxembourg!" "And I," replied Josephine, "am going to Iceland!"

But since the planes to Iceland and Luxembourg were scheduled to leave New York at the same time of day, the sisters agreed to drive to the airport together. When they arrived, they found several of their friends waiting for them. The friends had come to see the sisters off; they did so every year and always said farewell to both at once. But this year, since the sisters were going in separate directions, they had to do things differently: they had to say a first goodbye for Josephine and after that a separate bye for Kate.

So, whenever something (or someone) divides or separates into two parts, like Josephine and Kate, remember the friends who had to say a separate bye for Kate, and you will remember the word

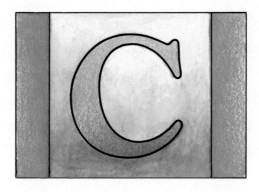

Mr. Efrem Sawdust, the manager of the Turkey Trotters Two Ring
Circus and Ice Capade, was looking for someone to replace the fat man
who had gone on a diet. "No more fat men for me," thought Mr. Sawdust,
as he chewed on the end of a cigar; "I'm going to find a glittering new act
to use in my circus." So Mr. Sawdust advertised in every newspaper,
inviting one and all to try out.

The day of the tryouts, dozens of people arrived at the circus: clowns,
tumblers, dancers, bareback riders, lion tamers, high-wire acrobats,
gymnasts, strongmen, animal trainers. "All right," shouted Mr. Sawdust,
chewing on his cigar, "let's get started. But remember, what I'm looking
for is a bright new act—one that glitters! So do your stuff!"

An elephant trainer led a great African elephant into the first circle. At
the trainer's command, the elephant jumped through a flaming hoop.
Then he spun around on one leg, balanced a beach ball on the end of his
trunk, and trumpeted "My Country 'Tis of Thee." "Yes, yes. Very good,"
said Mr. Sawdust. "But it's not quite what I had in mind."

A high-wire performer climbed to the top of the circus tent and, without a safety net below, walked across a wire suspended 100 feet above the ground. Then he walked to the middle of the wire, stopped, balanced on one foot, leaned over, and taking hold of the wire, performed a hand—stand. Mr. Sawdust shook his head. "Not bad. Not bad," he said. "But I already have a high-wire performer. I'm looking for something different—an act with sparkle and flash!"

Standing off to one side was an ice skater. "What are you doing here, kid?" said Mr. Sawdust. "I've come to try out," answered the girl. "Why," laughed Mr. Sawdust, "you couldn't be more than ten years old." "But I've been skating for eight years," she replied. "I'll give you two minutes," said Mr. Sawdust, chewing on the end of his cigar. The girl took a deep breath and swept out on the ice.

Quickly she skated from one end of the rink to the other, back and forth, over and over again, faster and faster; suddenly she jumped, spinning in midair, turning until she appeared, in the beam of the spotlight, to be floating suspended in air. Her spins and jumps were dazzling. Her loops and curves were glittering. Her costume was sparkling. The spray of ice, set free by her skidding skates, looked like puffs of smoke hanging in the shafts of light.

Mr. Sawdust was speechless. He couldn't believe his eyes. The girl glittered and gleamed; she sparkled and flashed. Mr. Sawdust was so amazed he did something he hardly ever did: he took his cigar out of his mouth. Calling the girl to the side of the rink, Mr. Sawdust exclaimed, "You're hired; what's your name, kid?" "Cora," she said. "You'll be famous, Cora; I'll put your name in lights." With a shake of his head, Mr. Sawdust relit his cigar and walked away mumbling. "What a performance! Boy, can that Cora skate!"

So, whenever you want to remember the word that means to glitter or gleam, to sparkle or flash, think of why Mr. Sawdust said, "Boy, can that Cora skate," and you will remember the word

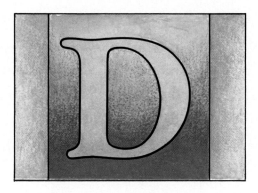

In the deep warm fur of a dog named Shadrack, there lived a family of ticks: a mother, a father, and their daughter, Polly. Now the ticks had a contented, happy home in Shadrack's fur. Shadrack never scratched himself, or rolled over, or took a bath. So the ticks enjoyed a close family life, until one day…

On that day, little Polly Tick climbed out of Shadrack's fur and snuggled into Shadrack's mat. Mother and Father Tick were very sorry that Polly had left to make a new home. "Come back," Mother and Father Tick called to Polly in their tiny voices. "Never," answered Polly, "I've decided that ticks should live in mats, and I think you should join me."

Polly's father could not understand. "What do you mean?" he asked. "Haven't we always lived in Shadrack's fur, and haven't we always been happy?" "Yes," Polly answered, "but mats, I think, are better than dogs. Mats do not run about in the cold. Mats do not bark. Mats are warm and still and quiet. They are the only place to live."

Polly's mother was deeply hurt and even ashamed. "How have I failed?" said her mother; "where did I go wrong? Young girls should not leave home before they marry. Your leaving will kill your grandmother."

"Grandmother," said Polly, "is as strong as a horse. She jogs a mile a day. You'll just have to explain that my home's in a mat." Polly's mother started to cry. "Think of me! she begged. "I'll call you every weekend," said Polly; "I promise."

"Maybe you'd be willing to try another dog?" said her father. "For instance, a long-haired terrier?" Polly said, "No!" "Then what about a short-haired terrier?" Polly said, "No!" "A poodle?" Polly said, "No!" Her father was crushed. "Isn't there anything I can do to convince you to come home?" he asked. Polly said, "No!" "Why?" asked her father. "Because," Polly answered, "I believe that I am right and you are wrong."

"And I believe," replied her father sternly, "that you are being stubborn and strong-willed! I see that you will never change your mind. There's no use reasoning with you, now that you've become a dog mat tick."

So, when people will not change their opinions because they are stubborn, like Polly, who left home to become a dog mat tick, those people are called

While the butterflies fluttered foolishly and the grasshoppers pranced playfully, the ants were busy collecting food for the bare, cold winter that they knew would be blowing down very soon from the hills. Every morning, they marched forth from their anthill and, in orderly fashion, broke into small hunting parties to find food. Ants, as we know, are hard workers, but some ants are stronger and faster than others. In this particular colony, there was one who was greatly admired by his fellows. Because he could gather food faster than any other ant, he was made Commander of the Fleet. He was so fast that his legs whirred like propellers. With the food clamped firmly in his jaws, he looked like a black streak as he whirred past the other ants.

With the smell of winter on the wind, the ants were hurrying to collect enough food to last until spring. The commander, as usual, was the hero of the anthill. He did the work of three ants, since he brought back three times as much food as anyone else. His feats of strength and speed were legendary. Parents told their children bedtime stories about him. Old folks compared him to the heroes of yesteryear.

When his friend said, "What's your secret?" he answered, "Exercise!" And to show that he meant what he said, he did push-ups and sit-ups each night and jogged at least five miles a day. He did jumping jacks, head-stands, toe-stands, windmills, hurdles, splits, knee-bends, side-bends, and neck-rolls. He ran in place. He stretched. He flexed. He pulled and pushed and rolled. And every day he seemed to run faster...

...Until one day, in late fall, a tree broke in a high wind. It fell across a stream and formed a bridge leading from the commander's meadow to a strange, new world. The commander crossed to the other bank and discovered a large wood structure, which people call a picnic table. When he looked underneath, he could not believe his eyes. The ground was covered with food. "This place must be paradise," he thought. He was so overcome by the richness of the bank that he lay down in the grass to catch his breath.

When he had recovered from his astonishment, he began to taste the food: a bite of cheese, a bit of bread, a taste of apple, a swallow of chocolate. In no time at all, the commander was stuffed. "Wow!" he thought, "what a feast. No more running for me. My running days are over. All I have to do is carry this food to the anthill and we'll be well-fed for a year." And that is exactly what he did. From the day of his discovery until the day he retired, the commander never ran again. He walked. He gave up his exercises; and he gave up his title as Commander of the Fleet. After all, why work so hard and run so fast to find food, when all he had to do was cross the stream and go to the picnic table?

Did he regret that he was no longer the fastest ant in the hill? "Not really," he said. "Once I was called a speedy ant; but now I'm happy to be called an ex-speedy ant."

So, when a person takes the easy way out, or does the practical or convenient thing—like the commander, who was content to be called an ex-speedy ant—we say that person is being

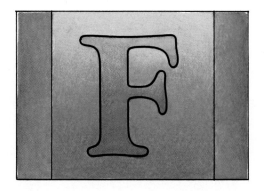

Woody Block was a dreamer. He wanted to build the perfect city—one that would make everyone who lived in it happy. His idea was simple: to build a city under the sea. There would be parks with paths winding through the coral and the gardens of seaweed. There would be submarine buses and a zoo filled with cages for sharks and stingrays and other strange and curious sea creatures. Instead of fountains of water in the public square, there would be air fountains that would release interesting patterns of bubbles through the clear green water. "Just imagine," he thought, "you could sit at a window and watch schools of brilliantly colored fish float by." He drew up his plans. But when he showed them to his friends they were puzzled. "There's just one problem, Woody," they said. "How are people going to live down there? How are they going to breathe?" Woody didn't know what to say. He hadn't thought of that.

Woody was not discouraged. He still dreamed about building a perfect city. So he read all the books in the library and found an idea for a new kind of city. He discovered that there was a special material that was as clear as glass and as strong as steel.

"That's it!" he shouted, "a glass city." He sat down immediately and drew a plan. Before the fall leaves had begun turning gold, the work began.

People came from miles around to watch as the strange glass-like buildings went up. When the city was built, newspapermen and photographers came from all over the world to see it. Sunlight gleamed through the walls and roofs. Rainbows of light splashed the street. Shining stairways led to towers that twinkled in the sun. And as day darkened, the colors of the city changed from bright yellow and blue to purple and orange. Woody smiled at the spectators and said, "I can hardly wait for the people to move into the city I've made for them." Suddenly, everyone was frowning. A photographer said, "I thought it was just art. You don't think people would really live here, do you? There wouldn't be any privacy." "That's right," said another, "I could see everything my neighbors were doing; and what's worse, they could see me." A woman added, "Oh my, I would have to keep my house clean all the time." Well, you can guess what happened. No one wanted to live in Woody's city. So although it became a famous work of art, it always remained empty.

But still Woody was not discouraged. He had a new idea: to build a city in the air. "I'll make a balloon city," he said. "It will be wonderful! It will float in the breeze! A city of birds and of clouds!" Once again, he set to work. He had workmen make the many platforms that were to hang by sturdy ropes from the balloons. On the platforms, they built light, plastic houses. Out of strong rubber, they made hundreds of colored balloons.

Then they roped the balloons together and filled them with gas. The city rose slowly into the sky. Suddenly, fierce gusts of wind struck the balloons, snarling and twisting the ropes, and shaking the platforms wildly. The balloons began to pop—and the whole city started to fall toward the ground. "Thank heaven, it's empty," said an old man. Everyone agreed that a balloon city was not a safe place to be in a storm.

Woody now knew that if he wanted to build a perfect city, he would have to think about people first. So he asked what made them happy. In almost every case, they answered: "Other people." Woody had learned his lesson: he built a city for people. Everyone was happy to live there; and, of course, Woody was happy, too—because he had finally come to fill a city.

So, whenever a person has great happiness, like Woody, who finally came to fill a city, we call that happiness

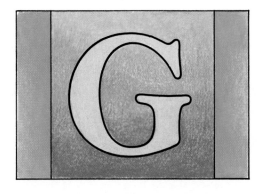

Dr. Emridge was new in town. Fresh out of medical school, he had come to "Last Breath," Minnesota to replace Dr. Gerald Shaygrin, who had practiced medicine in that town for fifty years.

The first morning in Last Breath, the new doctor went to introduce himself to Dr. Shaygrin.

"What's the most common complaint?" asked Dr. Emridge.

"Aching bones," answered Dr. Shaygrin. "When the mines gave out, only the old timers stayed behind."

Dr. Emridge rubbed the side of his nose and said, "How do you keep them going?"

"Well," said Dr. Shaygrin, "I'll tell you. A long time ago I discovered that old folks were just like anyone else—they like to be entertained. So I learned a few tricks…"

Then the two men sat down next to the fireplace and Dr. Shaygrin told the following story.

"The first time I walked into the old folks' hospital ward, it was as quiet as night. No one talked. No one smiled. No one even noticed me. I knew then that something had to be done. Now, my granddaddy was a magician; and he taught me that magic is like poetry: for a brief moment it transforms the world and makes it appear as wonderful as it really is. So the next day I showed up at the hospital in three hats. 'See these hats?' I said, holding them up one at a time. 'You can see for yourself that there's nothing in them!' And I turned each hat upside down and shook it. Pretty soon, all the old folks were propping up their pillows and watching me. Then I set the hats down in a row on a table. Bending over the first hat, I said 'abracadabra' and pulled out a white rabbit, which I set loose on the floor. Bending over the second hat, I said 'shazam' and pulled out a frog, which I set loose on the floor. Bending over the third hat, I said 'Fee-fie-diddle-dee-dee' and pulled out a bird, which I set loose in the air. Before you could say 'Kick the can', the whole place was laughing and yelling, chasing the animals and trying to catch the bird. After that day, everyone knew my name. Whenever I'd come into the old folks' ward, the patients would shout, 'Perform for us, Gerry! Do a trick! Please, Gerry!' And I would, because when people have something to look forward to, they move ahead and improve."

Dr. Shaygrin stretched his legs and rubbed his hands in front of the fire. "That's the end of my story," he said.

Dr. Emridge was silent. Then, after a long pause, he said, "I wish I knew how to do tricks. I wish, Dr. Shaygrin, you'd teach me, so that I can take care of the old folks." "Of course I'll teach you," replied the old doctor. "I'll teach you how to do Gerry hat tricks."

So, whenever you want to remember the branch of medicine that involves the care of elderly people, remember Dr. Shaygrin and his Gerry hat tricks, and you will remember the word

Twenty-five hundred years ago in Greece, the people lived as their fathers had lived. Life changed very little from one generation to the next. The short pleated skirts, called chitons, that their parents wore, they wore. The marble temples that their ancestors built and worshipped in, they worshipped in. And the gods that their fathers prayed to, they prayed to.

Every morning, the men and women of Andrea Zaragata's family would go to the Temple of Zeus and, like their ancestors, give thanks to that great god. Lamps were lit, prayers were said, and ceremonies were performed. The men and women would call to Zeus, the father of the gods, if any injury or insult had gone unnoticed or unpunished.

"Oh Zeus," they would cry, "see the wickedness of our enemies." Or a husband, unhappy with his wife's behavior, might say, "Oh Zeus, see how my wife no longer obeys me." Or a wife, wishing to point out how her husband bullied her, might say, "Zeus, see!"

27

But although Zeus often answered the prayers of the men, he never seemed to answer the prayers of the women. When a Greek wife complained that her husband bullied her, Zeus ignored her. Why should he listen? Zeus himself bullied his own wife, Hera. All Mount Olympus rang with the shouting whenever he and Hera had an argument. "I am right," Zeus would storm, "because I am your husband!" "Bullies," Hera would respond, "don't deserve to be answered!"

Naturally, the wives were annoyed when Zeus ignored their prayers, but no one ever disagreed with him, until…

One day, Andrea Zaragata marched up to the Temple of Zeus and started to shout: "Zeus, why do you never see? Why do you never take my side?" Andrea was angry because she wanted to lengthen her chiton: but her husband would not let her, and Zeus would not persuade him. After waiting in front of the Temple of Zeus for a whole day and receiving no answer, Andrea did something that no woman in her family had ever done before: she prayed to Hera.

"Hera," she cried, thinking of the new style in chitons, "see how my husband prevents me from lowering my hem." And suddenly she was struck with an idea! Andrea would not clean the house until she got her way. Before long, Andrea's husband grew tired of dirty clothes, dirty dishes, dirty children. He agreed that Andrea could lengthen her chiton, if only she would look after the house.

Andrea was sure that Hera had answered her prayer. So from that day forth, she prayed only to Hera. She even advised the other women in her family to do the same thing. But they would not agree. They preferred to observe the traditional beliefs of their family. They brought their complaints to Zeus and not Hera, and never allowed themselves to say, "Hera, see!"

So, whenever you want to describe the beliefs of someone who has gone against the religion of her people, remember Andrea who stopped worshipping Zeus and prayed by saying, "Hera, see," and you will remember that such beliefs are called

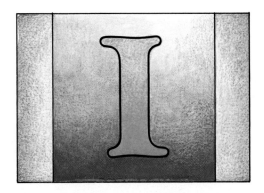

Poor and ugly Henrietta Brusselsnout wanted to get married, but she did not want to get married to just anybody. She wanted to marry Horatio Algermint, the famous millionaire. She liked Horatio's loud laugh, his big cigar, and his important voice. But most of all she liked his money. "Oh," she thought, "if only he would marry me, I would be rich. I would be richer than most kings and some oilmen." And because she wanted him to like her, she invited him to a wonderful dinner on Saturday night.

At six o'clock, Saturday night, Horatio Algermint knocked at the door. Henrietta opened it, and Horatio came in, saying "Hello, Hen! How are you?" "Just fine," she giggled, "just fine, Mr. Algermint. Do you like my new red dress?" Henrietta asked. "Well, not so much, to tell the truth. I never have liked red dresses," he said. "Oh," she cried, "I'll change it. I'll change it right away."

She hurried to her room and looked all through her closet. "There's my next best dress, the blue one," she said to herself. "I'll wear it." She ran back to Horatio. "Do you like my new blue dress?" "Well, not so much, to tell the truth. I never have liked blue dresses," he said. "Oh," she cried, "I'll change it. I'll change it right away."

She put on a yellow dress. He didn't like it. She put on a black dress. He didn't like it. She put on a green dress, then a white dress, then an orange dress. He didn't like any of them.

Finally, the only dress she had left was her old gray dress. She was ashamed to put it on, but she did anyway, and came back to Mr. Algermint, who was sitting in the living room. When he saw the gray dress, his eyes lit up.

"Well, well," he said, "I like that dress. I have always liked gray."

Together they went into the dining room to have dinner. As Horatio was drinking his tomato juice, he was thinking that Henrietta would make a good wife because she always tried very hard to please him. By the time the dessert came, Horatio had decided to ask Henrietta to be his wife. And so, Henrietta married Horatio, one of the richest men in the world, because in gray she ate.

So, whenever a person tries very hard to please someone, or tries to bring himself into favor with that person, think of Henrietta, who pleased Horatio because in gray she ate, and you will remember the word

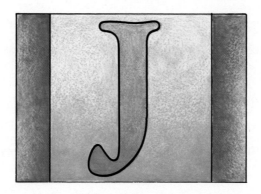

When the morning newspaper came, Mr. and Mrs. Dimple couldn't believe their eyes. Right on page one it said, "Wanted: a boy and a girl, ages 7 and 9, to star in a family show. Apply at FUN-TV, 3:00 to 6:00 today." Mr. Dimple was overjoyed. "There you are, Mrs. Dimple! Just what you've always wanted—a chance for our children to perform!" Mrs. Dimple was speechless, but only for a moment. "Who would believe it?" she said, "Our children are the perfect ages. Bobby is 7 and Barby is 9. And where in the world are there two children who can sing and dance and juggle spoons better than Bobby and Barby?" "Nowhere!" said Mr. Dimple. "Exactly!" said Mrs. Dimple. "I'll make an appointment for this afternoon."

As soon as Bobby and Barby returned from school, Mrs. Dimple took them to see Producer Slick. "Meet Bobby and Barby," cried Mrs. Dimple, as she paraded the children in front of the camera. "Believe me, you've never seen such talent. They're marvelous, simply marvelous. Why, they can dance and sing and whistle through their teeth. Just name it; they'll do anything you like."

"Well, actually," said Mr. Slick, "I'd like the children to sit down side by side in front of the camera, because in this show…" But before he could finish his sentence, Barby started to tap-dance. Her clattering shoes drowned out the producer, who barely could make himself heard: "You don't understand!"

Barby had no sooner finished her dance than Bobby began to sing. "Sweet and Low," he hollered, "Sweet and Low!" His voice grew louder and louder, until the producer covered his ears. "Does he always turn bright purple when he sings!" asked Mr. Slick. "Always," said Mrs. Dimple proudly; "perfect for color TV, don't you think?"

"Please, Mrs. Dimple, you must understand!" pleaded Mr. Slick. "This is a family show! The children have to appear side by side, as if playing a game…" "If it's games you want," interrupted Mrs. Dimple, "then it's games you'll get! Juggle your spoons, children!" Reaching into his pocket, Bobby removed eight silver spoons, threw them high overhead, and leap-frogged with Barby beneath the flying silverware. The children then bounced to their feet and reached for the spoons—which crashed to the floor.

"Enough!" shouted Mr. Slick. "Won't you do as I ask and sit next to each other? Stop singing and dancing and juggling spoons. Sit down on this bench and remain side by side. I'll ask you once more: can I have just a pose?"

So, whenever you want to remember the word that means to place side by side, remember Mr. Slick asking for "just a pose," and you will remember the word

Juxtapose

In one of the wide and windy valleys of high Tibet, there was a little snow-swept village. The weather was often bitterly cold, especially when the wind, heavy with snow, swept down the northern peaks. The people in their huts would huddle around small fires, and the animals in their sheds would press against the walls for protection against the driving snow. No one was warm in winter except those whose clothes had been made from the fur of yaks. No wonder, then, the yaks were greatly valued.

During a very severe winter, Chutzpah, one of the villagers, could stand the cold no longer. Severe winters can, as we know, do strange things to people. Confined month after month to their homes and cabins, people often begin to go crazy. Such was the case with Chutzpah: his mind seemed to snap. He took from his toolshed a pair of shears and, when the moon had fallen behind the mountain and the clouds had covered the stars, he crept outside.

Following the crooked mountain path behind the village, he silently ran until he reached the barn where farmer Chungpa kept his yaks. Entering the barn, Chutzpah removed the shears from his pocket, clipped the fur from one of farmer Chungpa's yaks, and stuffed it into his jacket. Then he left the barn and followed the mountain path back to his house.

The next day, farmer Chungpa complained bitterly to the village elder, who was the chief man. "Somebody has stolen a mane from one of my yaks," cried farmer Chungpa. "The fur is very valuable. I want to make a coat." But what could the village elder do? No one knew who had stolen the mane from one of farmer Chungpa's yaks. After several days of asking questions, the village elder gave up the search. Chutzpah was safe. No one suspected him. He was delighted. He had not been caught; and the thought of taking something without being caught made his blood race and his heart pound. He suddenly knew that he would never be able to stop stealing!

It was all very sad. Chutzpah had enough money to buy a mane or a dozen manes. But the thought of stealing made him drunk with excitement—so he stole again and again and again, until he couldn't stop stealing manes. It was as though a disease had swept over him. Except that now, instead of stealing from farmer Chungpa, he stole from all the villagers. At least once a week, he entered a farmer's barn, clipped off a mane, and cleverly concealed it under his bed. When he wasn't stealing, he was dreaming of stealing.

The village elder decided to set a trap to catch the thief. The farmers were to bring their yaks to the center of the village and leave them overnight in a specially constructed pen. When Chutzpah saw the yaks, he couldn't control himself. As soon as night came, he took his shears and crept into the pen. Suddenly a dozen lanterns were lit. Chutzpah was surrounded. The thief was caught.

Brought before the village elder, Chutzpah was told that he would have to go to jail. The village elder said, "What I don't understand, Chutzpah, is why you stole. You have enough money to buy all the manes you want. Why did you do it?" Chutzpah, who was deeply ashamed, didn't know what to say. Finally he answered: "I couldn't help myself. The thought of stealing made me drunk. I couldn't help but clip the mane of yak."

So, whenever a person has an uncontrollable urge to steal, especially to steal things that he can afford to buy, remember Chutzpah, who had an irresistible urge to clip the mane of yak, and you will remember that such a person is called a

Kleptomaniac

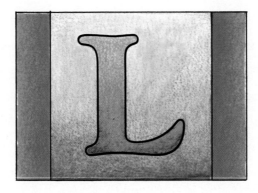

The people who lived in Slack City had always been the laziest and most forgetful people in the country. Sometimes they went to work, and sometimes they didn't. In the morning, if they got out of bed at all, they would brush their front teeth, and then quit; they would comb one side of their head, but not the other. They wore whatever clothes were lying around, never bothering to match their socks, or even their shoes. The children were almost always late for school. But the teachers didn't notice, because they never remembered to wind the school clocks.

In every street, there were empty cars that the owners had left because they had run out of gas. No one remembered to turn off his garden hose, so the streets were always flooded. Lawns were never cut and grew to be as high as the corn. Flowers were smothered in weeds. The trashmen left piles of dirt here and there along the curbs. The library forgot to order books. The hospital was closed: someone had lost the key to the front door. In summertime, the mosquitoes invaded every house because all the screens were torn; and in wintertime, since no one ever changed worn-out light bulbs, everyone lived in darkness.

The townspeople were so lazy that when the great hurricane of 1947 blew down the sign that read SLACK CITY, it took them ten years to collect enough money to build a new one. But no sooner was the money collected than it was lost. And no sooner was it found than it was lost again. After looking in attics and basements and cookie jars, the townspeople finally found the money in the Mayor's lunch pail.

In January, the local handyman was summoned to build the sign, but work did not begin until June, since he had misplaced his saw and paint-brush. On a warm summer day, he drove an old truck to the edge of town, where the sign was to be built. From the truck he unloaded ladders, saws, hammers, nails, buckets of paint, and a dozen boards. He also unloaded a tent, pots and pans, a sleeping bag, and food—because any job that should normally have taken one day to do took three days in Slack City.

When the handyman had nailed together all the boards, he climbed a ladder, took a paintbrush, and started to paint the name of the city in large block letters. After he had finished the lettering, some townspeople, who had been watching, called out to him and said: "You forgot the S. It's supposed to say Slack City," The handyman shrugged his shoulders and answered: "Oh, well, it doesn't matter very much, does it?"

The townspeople thought for a minute about what he had said. Then they yawned and walked away, saying as they went, "No, we don't care; one way's as good as another. Let it say Lack City,"

So, when people are careless and forgetful, like the handyman who forgot the S in "Lack City," such people are known for their

Harry Jailbird was always causing trouble. He was mean, and nasty, and could never be trusted. He pulled the tails of cats, kicked dogs, rubbed candlewax across car windows, and wrote bad words in wet cement. No one liked him; but Harry didn't care. A long time ago, he had decided to misbehave. And one day in summer, he decided something worse: to break the law.

As he was passing City Hall, he saw a sign: "Keep off the grass," it said. "Why should I keep off?" said Harry to himself. And he marched across the grass right into the flower bed, crushing the violets and the peonies and the snapdragons. The town gardener had taken half the summer to grow those flowers, and Harry had spoiled them in a minute. No wonder the gardener was angry. No wonder he called the police.

But before the police could come, Harry marched down Main Street, grumbling and scowling and looking for trouble. He reached the corner of Main and Ash just as the light turned red. "Why should I stop?" growled Harry. And he stepped into the street. Cars screeched to a halt. Horns honked. One car even crashed into another. It was all Harry's fault. No wonder the drivers were angry. No wonder they called the police.

But before the police could come, Harry walked into a corner grocery store. He took a sandwich from the shelf and a soda from the cooler, and ate them on the spot. "Why should I pay?" snarled Harry, as he passed the grocer at the cash register. "Why should you pay?" repeated the grocer; "because you've eaten my food, that's why!" Harry just made an ugly face and walked out of the store, right into the arms of Policeman Stern.

"You're under arrest," cried the policeman, who took out a pair of handcuffs and put them on Harry. "Mean cop," muttered Harry, not one little bit ashamed of himself.

48

"Mean, am I!" asked Policeman Stern. "Well, you may think I'm mean. But let me tell you: you're the one who walked on the grass and stepped on the flowers and crossed the street on a red light. And you're the one who caused a car to crash and robbed the grocer by stealing a sandwich and soda. If you think I'm mean, what about you? Given the things you've done today, you are, mister, meaner."

So, whenever someone has broken the law, remember Policeman Stern saying to Harry Jailbird, "you are, mister, meaner," and you will remember that a lawless act is called a

It had not rained for a month, so the great witch doctor ordered his tribe to perform the rain dance. From the first drum beats—just as the Indians started their circling dance—huge black clouds appeared overhead and the air was filled with rain. After a short time, the dancers had to stop because the feathers in their headdresses drooped with water, and their feet were wet and muddy. By the next day everything was soaking wet. But the rain went on and on. It put out the watchfires, flooded the wigwams, and ran through the streets. And still it rained, until all the Indians had terrible colds. They blew their noses, coughed, and then blew their noses again. Finally, the Indians could stand it no more. Sniffling and snorting, they went to the Witch Doctor and with croaking voices cried, "Heal us, oh Great One!"

Now the Witch Doctor, though he tried to seem wise, was really quite silly. All round his wigwam he had hung old bones, scraps of beaded leather, and weeds, which he called magic herbs. These things, he said, had secret powers; and only he knew the words to unlock their magic.

50

Narrowing his eyes to look mysterious, he listened to the tribesmen's complaints about their colds. Then, stroking his chin, he replied in a strange, low voice, "Your great drums have summoned the spirits of the sky. And the spirits of the sky have flown up your noses and given you colds. To drive out the evil spirits from your noses, you must use little drums." Then he told the Indians to go into the forest and build tiny tom-toms. When they returned, he said, "Instead of pounding the drums with your hands, you must use your noses."

All day long, the Indians squatted before their drums, rocking back and forth, banging the ends of their noses on the tiny tom-toms. The drums sounded very strange, but even stranger was the sight of the Indians sitting on the ground beating drums with their noses.

Did the little drums work? Probably not, but the Indians' noses were so sore from beating them that they completely forgot about their colds. The Witch Doctor, of course, took credit for curing the Indians. He went around the village bragging loudly: "I am a great Witch Doctor. I heal the wounded and cure the sick. When the rains came and our people caught cold, it was I who told them to go into the forest and build tiny tom-toms." Although he had not really cured them, the Witch Doctor always said that the Indians had recovered from their colds because of the nose-drums.

So, whenever you want to describe a cure that does not really work, think of the Indians beating their tiny nose-drums, and you will remember the word

Nostrum

There once lived a sparrow by the name of Sidney. Now, Sidney was different from all the other sparrows in his family. Sidney, you see, was six feet tall. His mother and father and brothers and sisters and cousins and aunts and uncles were only three inches tall. Sidney was very proud of his size. Every day he would brag that he was the tallest sparrow in the world. He would compare himself to the ostriches, whom he admired, and boast about the things he could do.

"I can reach the branches of trees," he said. "I can look over tall hedges. I can, before anyone else, see the morning sun and the evening moon—and feel the autumn rain and the winter snow. All things that come from heaven reach me before they reach you."

When company came to visit, Sidney Sparrow would say, "You are so short, you can shake hands with the groundhog and dine with the mole. You must eat the berry from the thorn bush and the root from the ground. In the company of other birds you are no taller or shorter than most. Now I am as tall as the ostriches. Don't you wish you were as tall as I?"

Sidney even said to his school friends, "Don't you wish that you could roam with the ostriches as I do? We run together in the grasslands, take our meals under acacia bushes, bathe in cold rivers, and stand watch for the lion. You are not my brothers. The ostriches are my brothers."

One day, Sidney Sparrow's mother and father could no longer stand to hear him brag about being as tall as the ostriches. So they told him that he would have to leave the family and go away. Sidney did not understand. "If it gives me pleasure to run with the ostriches," he said, "why should you mind?" His father answered, "We are glad that you like the ostriches, but we are sad that you use this friendship to make fun of the sparrows." Sidney was shocked: "You would send me away?" His father replied, "I would send you away." Sidney said, "I must leave?" His mother replied, "You must leave!"

Sidney Sparrow was not happy to leave his mother and father, and all the other sparrows. He did not like being shut out from his family—and all because he bragged about his unusual ostrich-size.

So, whenever a person (or bird) has been deliberately left out or excluded from a group, think of Sidney, who was sent away from home because he bragged about his unusual ostrich-size, and you will remember the word

Once in the middle of the great polar jungles, an explorer discovered a strange and beautiful valley. In this place, between two mountains, rivers ran uphill, the sun rained, and fire was icy cold. Birds barked in the trees, cats chased dogs, fish flew through the air, and the lion and lamb lay down together. For five days the explorer walked through the valley. As the meadow grasses gave way to marshlands, he could see beasts of white plumage and birds of bay bloom. And as the highlands passed into the jungle, he could hear the chatter of snakes and see the shadow of fish. The explorer had come to the polar jungles not only to map uncharted lands, but also to find rare animals.

On the seventh day, as the explorer was pushing his way through swamplands and thick jungle undergrowth, he heard a loud, screeching sound above him. Looking up, he saw, of all things, a lake in a tree. In the middle of the lake a most wonderful animal was looking at him and squawking:

Stranger, stranger in the bush
Be very careful where you push.
In the jungle there's no path
Between the high ground and the bath.

One step here, and one step there—
The swamp is foul, the jungle's fair.
So be alert, look around,
Step to the air and miss that ground.

The explorer leaped to one side—just missing a pit, filled with bubbling quicksand, rolling and shaking, slowly swallowing itself until only the sound remained.

"Thank you," shouted the explorer. "But who are you, and what are you doing here?" The animal splashed about in the tree and babbled:

Beasts of the air and birds of the sea
Reside in a word and not in a tree.
If my rigamarolery seems to be dense,
Remember that poetry always makes sense.

"It's amazing!" the explorer said to himself; "It's simply incredible!"

The animal had a head like a bird, wings covered with feathers of every color, an enormous cow-like body, and four huge legs with hoofs. It was a parrot—and at the very same time it was an ox.

"Who will ever believe that I've seen such an animal?" thought the explorer. "People will say it's impossible; they'll say this creature cannot exist!" But nevertheless there it was, sitting in the middle of a lake in a tree, flapping its wings, shaking its big belly, and chattering:

> Half-bird, half-beast, and a chatterbox,
> A wonderful thing is a parrot-ox.

So, whenever something seems impossible at first, but turns out to be true, like a parrot-ox, we call that thing a

Dick was a carpenter and something of a dreamer. He lived in a small town in New Jersey called Shoutsville. He loved being a carpenter because it gave him the opportunity to work with his hands. Nothing gave him more joy than measuring a length of wood, sawing it, and nailing it in place. In just a couple of hours he could build a chair; in a week he could build a cabinet; in a month, a house.

Now the small town that Dick lived in was a pretty place, with a river of dark cedar water running through the middle of town. The only trouble was that the people of Shoutsville were always shouting at one another for no reason at all. Dick was ashamed of the way his neighbors behaved. "Why can't they get along?" he thought. "I must think of something to make them stop shouting at one another." Being a dreamer, Dick was convinced that every problem has its solution—if only the solution can be found. While working in his shop one morning, he had an idea: "I will make a handsome wooden chair for every person in Shoutsville. Then the people will be happy, and stop shouting at one another." So he set to work immediately to build 75 chairs for the 75 people who lived in Shoutsville.

The chairs were designed for comfort and beauty. Dick was a first-rate craftsman. Everyone said so. When he drove his pickup into town, with the chairs neatly stacked in the back, the people wondered at the sight and gathered round. "My good people of Shoutsville," Dick said, "I have dreamed of making you friendly by building you comfortable chairs. The ones you have at home have made you moody and grouchy, so you shout at your neighbors. But now I have brought you comfortable chairs. Now no one has to shout; no one has to yell. Now everyone can be friends." The people clapped and thanked Dick for all his hard work.

But as he was taking the chairs from the truck, Dick could hear people murmuring, "His chair is darker than mine"; or "her chair is lighter than mine"; or "the wood in his chair has a prettier grain than mine"; or "the finish on her chair is smoother than mine." Even before the truck was unloaded, the murmurs had turned to shouts. "Don't fight," Dick said; "I'll go back to my shop and build all of you comfortable beds and tables, desks and chairs—if only you'll stop shouting at one another." The people mumbled something about "being sorry" and "trying harder next time." Then they took the chairs and went home.

The next day, Dick set to work with desperate energy and speed. He sawed twice as fast as before. His workshop quickly filled with beds, tables, and chairs. But no matter how much furniture he gave away, the people of Shoutsville continued to fight. No one paid any attention to Dick's dream. Only one thing happened. Because Dick worked so hard and sawed so fast, the people of Shoutsville began to call him Quick-Saw Dick.

So, whenever a person dreams an impossible dream, a dream that cannot come true because it is not possible or practical, think of Quick-Saw Dick, and you will remember that impractical dreamers, like Dick, are called

Leonard Lyon was a soft-spoken, gentle lion. He drank water and not whiskey; he chewed gum instead of tobacco. He liked the other cats and never kicked dogs. He was good to his parents. And never, no never, not even once, did he get into a fight or growl loudly. Still, Tina Tiger, the girl Leonard loved, could not make up her mind whether to marry Leonard Lyon or Jerry Jaguar, the loud cat who always shouted hoarsely in anything but polite language.

Jerry, in fact, was a terrible cat. For no good reason at all, he would swear and cuss and yell and curse. Often he would growl so loudly that, for miles around, the valleys would echo. He complained noisily if the day was too hot or too cold, if the grass was too long or too short, if the elephants were too loud or the giraffes too quiet. Why, he would yell if anyone even crossed his shadow. Nothing escaped his loud mouth.

Leonard Lyon, on the other hand, never used bad language. He would occasionally complain, of course, like anyone else, but always in the most polite manner. On a bad day, he might blurt out, "Oh, whips and wheels," or "Oh, crickets," or "Oh, sticks and stones"; but he would never say anything worse.

One fine spring morning, Tina Tiger suggested that the three of them take a picnic lunch to the racetrack, to see the gazelles run. So they left the forest and went to picnic on the infield grass at the racetrack. Tina brought a delicious lunch. But no sooner had they sat down than Jerry started to complain. "Hot dogs," he shouted at Tina, "you know I don't like hot dogs! Give me some hamburgers." Tina was silent, thinking to herself, "if he's going to behave like an ape, I'll just send him back to the forest."

Leonard Lyon, of course, was a perfect gentleman. He thanked Tina for the cole slaw, and the potato chips, and the pickles. He raved about the hot dogs and loved the relish. When Jerry complained, Leonard said, "Come on, Jerry, cheer up." But Jerry only shouted, "I hate sesame seed buns!"

For dessert, Tina gave each one a large piece of apple pie. But Jerry was unhappy. "Is there something wrong, Jerry?" Tina asked. "Where's the ice cream?" Jerry cried. "I don't eat apple pie without ice cream!" And he let loose a string of cuss words: ##$••–&&–•##$•–**!!! No one said anything for a long time. Then, after devouring his piece of apple pie in two swallows, Jerry loudly said, "I prefer cheese cake." Tina was almost in tears.

"The first race is starting!" yelled Jerry. "I've bet 100 coconuts on number 3 to win." But number 3 did not win; number 5 won. Jerry yelled and raged and fumed and swore: *#$•–)(#$•–##**#•*#©#*!!! By the end of the day he had lost all his coconuts, and his complaining turned to hoarse cussing. Jerry thundered at the heavens, cursed at the gazelles, and swore at his bad luck.

Leonard, on the other hand, was well-behaved. He, too, had lost all his coconuts, but he never once raised his voice. The worst things he ever said were "Oh, blushes and blooms" and "Oh, frogs and fishes."

Tina Tiger had finally had enough of Jerry's noisy behavior. She took Leonard Lyon by the arm and, turning to Jerry, said, "You can just go back to the forest by yourself. I am going to marry Leonard!" "Why?" he roared, "What have I done to deserve this?" Tina answered, "You have been loud and boisterous—and you cuss." "Really, Tina!" shouted Jerry, "what's a cuss word or two between friends?" Tina threw back her head and said, "Polite swearing is one thing, Jerry Jaguar; but you, in fact, are all raw cuss."

So whenever someone is loud and noisy and harsh-sounding, like Jerry Jaguar, who was all raw cuss, we say that person is being:

After years of misbehaving, the fireflies decided to correct their ways. Glum, the most dull-lighted of them, became their leader and buzzed on and on about the wickedness of their former lives. Glowing with anger, he spoke of the late hours they kept, of their showy flying, of their shameless twinkling. "Late hours," he said, "are for fireflies who don't care about their good name. Just think of all the terrible things that occur late at night. Showy flying is a sign of pride—and pride is what causes a firefly to fall into the mouth of a fine feathered fiend. Shameless twinkling is like showing off; it calls attention to itself, when one should be modest and humble." All of the fireflies who heard Glum speak agreed to change their lives. "From now on," they said, "we will keep proper hours, fly in decent style, and allow ourselves only the most soft and modest glow."

But changing their old ways was harder for some than for others. After a few nights of trying to follow the new rules, Gloriana Firefly swished her green light impatiently and said, "Oh, bother! Oh, nonsense! I shall do what I have always done!"

Then she flew off into the evening air. She soared. She circled. She twisted. She dove. Spinning and turning, wheeling and gliding, she lit up the sky with her dazzling flying. What a show-off! So brilliant were her light-streaks across the black sky that she seemed to be giving off flakes of fire or droplets of stars. She continued until the first light of dawn dimmed both the Milky Way and her, and she crawled off to sleep, weary but happy.

Night after night, long after the other fireflies had snuffed out their gleams, Gloriana repeated her sparkling performance. The other fireflies huddled on a tree branch and jealously watched her. "Simply shocking!" said one. "Disgraceful!" murmured a second. "Something should be done about that sinful creature!" said a third, tapping his tiny feet angrily. After seven nights of watching Gloriana show off, Glum said at last, "Gloriana will never stop misbehaving. She is a bad influence on the children. The other fireflies must not be allowed in her company. Let us fly away. Besides, we have better things to do with our time than watch that wicked Gloriana sin till late."

So, whenever a person (or thing) sparkles, or twinkles, or gives off light, think of Gloriana, who loved to sin till late, and you will remember the word

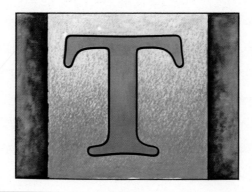

Hugh Crackenblock was a garage mechanic. But unlike some mechanics who can do only minor engine repairs, Hugh worked on the most difficult motors. In his garage, cranky, bumpy buses were made to run as smoothly as monorail cars; coughing, sputtering automobiles were made to travel as quietly as Paris subway trains; meek, little trucks were made as strong as jet airplanes. People from all over the country brought Hugh their sick cars and buses and trucks.

From one season to the next, Hugh turned broken-down engines into youthful hot rods, until one day Hugh met his match. A burly truck driver named Mack drove into Hugh's garage. Now, Mack's truck had a terrible temper. It was so fierce and violent that it would go down the highway honking at cars, bullying buses, cutting off trucks, and terrifying everyone on the road. "You have to repair this savage truck of mine!" Mack cried; "it's ruining my life. Every driver from New York to San Francisco hates me. The other truck drivers make fun of me because I can't make my truck behave. Every time I pull onto the road, I get a ticket."

Hugh shook his head and started to work. But whatever he did, the truck still growled. It snapped and barked. It coughed and sputtered. It charged down the road and pushed everyone out of its way. When Mack came to pick up his truck, Hugh said, "I'm sorry, I can't make your truck behave." Mack, of course, was very sad. He knew that it was too dangerous to take his truck out on the road again. So Mack left it on Hugh's parking lot. And there it stood for many months, ignored and unused.

It might, in fact, be standing there to this day, if a friend of Hugh's—Farmer Jack—had not met with an accident. The farmer's truck had broken down on the very day he had to drive his peaches to market. So he came to Hugh and asked to use the truck that was standing in the corner of the parking lot.

At first, Hugh absolutely refused. He explained, "Listen, Jack, that truck is fierce and bad tempered. You could get hurt driving it." But Jack pleaded, saying, "My peaches, Hugh, think of my peaches!" In the end, Hugh gave in.

Jack climbed into the truck and turned the key. The motor started. It was idling gently. "There's nothing to worry about," thought Jack; "I can hardly hear the engine." Then suddenly, to his surprise, the truck with a great roar, shot down the road. After months of standing, the truck was more fierce than ever. It chased cars into ditches; it tore the fender off a bus; it dented the rear end of a truck. Jack was scared to death. The truck was throwing a tantrum! Suddenly, it slid on a patch of oil, bounded off a guardrail, hit a telephone pole, blew two tires, skidded off a bridge, and landed upside down in a creek bed.

When Policeman Moonshine arrived on the scene, he yelled at Jack, "How dare you drive so recklessly?" Jack was silent. "Are you crazy, Jack? What's wrong with you?" he asked. "I've never seen you so fierce and savage." Jack stared at his feet and felt a lump rise in his throat. He tried to speak, but couldn't. He wanted to remind Policeman Moonshine that he was not a violent man, but a mild-mannered farmer who had been taken for a brutal ride by a vicious truck. "Cat got your tongue?" asked Policeman Moonshine. In a meek voice, Jack answered, "Policeman Moonshine, you know I'm not savage. The savage one is the truck Hugh lent."

So, whenever you want to describe someone who is fierce, or cruel, or savage, remember the truck Hugh lent, and you will remember the word

Because Urldemar Bagshot had such a difficult name, people called him U.B. They also called him dishonest. And for good reason: he never paid his bills. He would, for example, order expensive things from the best shops— things like diamond rings, fur coats, tape recorders, cameras, cars, skis, watches, silver tea sets, and gold candlesticks—and not pay for them. The stores would send him first one bill, then a second, and then a third. But he would just shrug his shoulders and throw the bills into the wastebasket. The store owners finally became so angry that they had U.B. arrested and brought to court.

When Judge Lynch heard about U.B.'s behavior, he was very stern. He ordered U.B. to get a job and pay his bills. "Take your pick," said Judge Lynch, "a job or jail!" "I'll take a job," said U.B., thinking that he would fool the judge by only pretending to look for work. But the judge would not be fooled. "Good," he said, "You can start tomorrow—as a clerk in the law office of my good friends Murphy, Goldberg, and Clark."

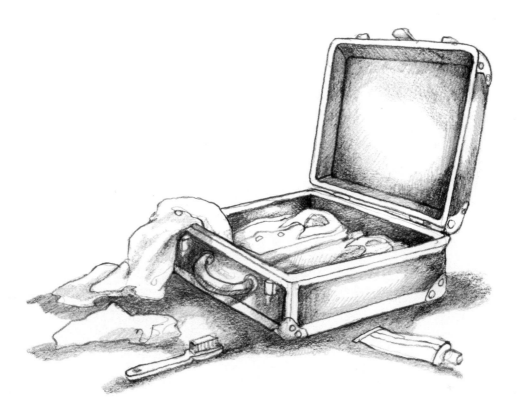

Now what was U.B. to do? It wasn't just that he was lazy. He absolutely, totally, completely, wholly, and utterly hated to work. So he decided to run away. After a month on the job, he packed his suitcase and hitched a ride to the train station. He boarded the 1:55 P.M. express to Boston, took a window seat, and stared into the neighboring train. To U.B.'s surprise, he found himself face to face with Judge Lynch. The Judge pointed his finger and started to shout. But U.B. couldn't hear a word; he just smiled and tipped his hat, as the trains slowly pulled out of the station.

"Impossible!" thought Judge Lynch. "I couldn't have been looking at Urldemar Bagshot. He's at work! It's 1:55 in the afternoon! When I return from Philadelphia, I'm going to visit Murphy, Goldberg, and Clark to find out for myself…"

The next day, Judge Lynch called on his friends. "Where was U.B. yesterday?" asked the Judge. "I sent him to the library," said Mr. Murphy. "To the library?" asked Mr. Goldberg; "I sent him to the courthouse." "To the courthouse?" said Mr. Clark; "I sent him to the post office." "Remarkable," said the Judge; "I thought I saw him on the train to Boston. How could he have been in four places at once?" "I can only conclude," said Mr. Clark, "that yesterday, U.B. quit us."

So whenever you want to describe a person who appears to be everywhere at once, remember Mr. Clark explaining that "Yesterday, U.B. quit us," and you will remember that such a person is called

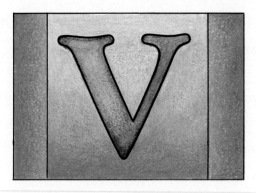

One frosty morning in March, when King Numeral was having his breakfast, he received a report that the Kingdom of Numberland was about to be attacked. King Numeral held a hasty council with the highest numbers of the court. "Prince Maxi-million," the King said, "what battle plan do you suggest we follow?" Prince Maxi-million answered, "I think the best way to handle numbers is to divide them. My lancers will be placed at the edge of the woods to attack from the north; and my foot soldiers will cross the river and attack from the west." "Very good," said the King.

Baron 61, who had been sitting quietly, jumped to his feet and said, "For this great cause, I pledge all my gold and my castles to help pay the costs of war. After all, every man must be willing to help at a time like this." The King was very pleased to receive such cooperation from his court.

He then turned to Vassal 99 and said, "Let your men be the first to take the field of battle."

That afternoon, there was feverish activity in the castle yard. The vassals, who are lords with special duties to the King, were being organized by Vassal 99 to lead the troops to battle. Duke 85 was giving out weapons: swords, shields, knives, picks, crossbows, and lances. The Counts, being the most devoted to the cause, were, of course, keeping track of how much money was being spent and who owed what to whom. And the subjects of the land, from the simply clothed Ciphers to the most splendid Numerals, were eagerly awaiting battle.

Soon, everyone was ready to meet the enemy—everyone, that is, except for a vassal named 8. Now 8 was not at all sure that he wanted to fight. Whenever he looked at his bright armor, he longed for battle. Whenever he thought of the enemies' swords, he longed for bed. When he remembered his King and country, he reached for his lance. When he remembered his skin and bones, he reached for his cup of ale. He put his head in his hands and mumbled, "To go? To stay? To fight or not to fight? What shall I do?" He thought and thought.

At the end of the day, the Numberland Army marched to meet the enemy. But 8 was still in his room, uncertain whether to go or stay—mumbling to himself, "Maybe yes, and maybe no; perhaps I will, and perhaps I won't. I think I'll fight, and then again, I think I'll hide." One minute he was decided, and the next he was undecided. "I'll go! Or…maybe I won't," said Vassal 8.

So, whenever a person can't make up his mind about something and wavers from side to side, think of Vassal 8, and you will remember the word

The Mayor of Wigglesworth had ten children—all girls—and not one of them made any attempt to be pleasant or cheerful. They were all rude, loud, jealous, and quarrelsome. And yet the Mayor loved them dearly. He spoiled them with gifts and never tired of telling his friends how well-behaved his children were. In fact, the Mayor was so convinced of their charms that every year he entered one of his daughters in the "Wigglesworth City Personality Contest"; and every year she won first prize.

Now, you ask, how could this be? The answer is simple. The Mayor was the most influential man in Wigglesworth City, and none of the judges for the "Personality Contest" wanted to offend him. Also, the Mayor was not shy, especially when it came to promoting the interests of his daughters. He would go to see the three judges *before* the contest was held and say something like this: "Now, gentlemen, how long have we known one another and lived in this town as friends? Twenty years? Or is it thirty years? Well, however long it's been, it's been a long time. Right? Right!

And in all that time haven't I done you a favor or two? Maybe even five or six? Well, now I want you to do a favor for me. One of my daughters is entering the 'Personality Contest' and I want her to win first prize. She's a lovely girl. Don't you agree? Of course you agree. Good. Then it's done." Every year it was the same: one of the Mayor's daughters was awarded first prize.

But this year, an especially pleasant young lady by the name of Mary Marigold had entered the "Personality Contest." When the Mayor went to see the judges to ask them to award first prize to his daughter Goffa, a strange thing happened: the judges paused and coughed and cleared their throats and would not, as they had in the past, definitely say "Yes." "What's going on here?" the Mayor asked. "Are you or aren't you going to crown my beautiful daughter Goffa as queen of the 'Wigglesworth City Personality Contest'?" One of the judges replied, "First, we must inter- view the young ladies." The Mayor answered, "Go ahead and interview them—just as long as my Goffa wins first prize." Then he left, slamming the door behind him.

The interviews were held. Mary Marigold displayed a lovely voice and exhibited perfect manners. Goffa, on the other hand, entered the judges' room and said, "Hurry up, let's get this interview over with. We all know who's going to win the contest. So ask your questions and give me the prize. If you don't, I'll have my father fire you." When the first judge asked, "Where do you go to school?" Goffa answered, "What's it to you?" When the second judge asked, "What are you studying?" Goffa responded, "I hate school." And when the third judge inquired, "What do you intend to do after you leave school?" Goffa replied, "Nothing."

As soon as Goffa left the room, the first judge summoned up his courage and said to the others, "This state of affairs simply won't do. There must be a change." "But we have always given first prize to the Mayor's daughters," said the second judge. "Yes," said the third, "and in doing so we have ignored some lovely young ladies—for the Mayor's sake. This year we must do what's fair. Mary Marigold must win first prize." "You're right," said the second judge, "it's not fair to keep the other girls from winning." So Mary Marigold received first prize. And when the Mayor complained, the judges said his daughters had always won the prizes and now the time had come for pleasant girls to win some.

So, when anyone is charming, attractive, cheerful, and bright, like Mary Marigold, whose winning personality and smile persuaded the judges that pleasant girls deserved to win some, we say that person is

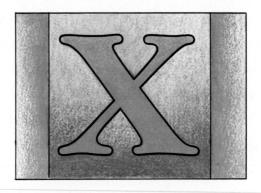

The Home Town Cafe was a friendly place—for the people in the neighborhood. But if any stranger, or any outsider, dropped in on the "Home Town," well…that was something else. When people from a different part of town came to eat at the cafe, the regular customers would look out of the corners of their eyes and mutter to their friends: "Who invited them? Where are they from? What strange birds!"

One Friday evening, the "Home Town" regulars were crowding around a television set and watching the local football game. Someone was yelling, "Kick the ball! What are you waiting for—kick the ball!" Someone else was waving his fist at the television set and shouting, "Pass it; pass it; he's wide open!" And still others were jumping up and down and shouting, "Tackle him! Don't let him get away!" During this excitement, the front door of the Home Town Cafe opened and four strangers walked in. They were foreigners—people from a different country. Suddenly the cafe was silent.

After a minute or two, someone pointed at the foreigners and whispered, "Look at those clothes! Did you ever see anything so ridiculous in your life? What are they wearing—sheets?" Then another whispered, "Look at their faces! They don't look like anyone from around here." Then a third whispered, "I bet they smell funny—because they sure look funny!"

The four foreigners sat down at a table. The owner of the Home Town Cafe—a man by the name of Buster Offenbach, nicknamed Buzz Off—walked over to the foreigners and said, "Yea, what d'ya want?" "It is O.K. zat we sit at zis table?" asked one of the foreigners. "Huh?" said Buzz. The foreigner repeated the question. Buzz couldn't believe his ears. He turned to the regulars and said, "Did you ever...? They can't even speak English!" The regulars began to laugh.

Then Buzz asked the foreigners again, "What d'ya want?" The foreigner who was doing the talking replied, "Vee vud, pleez, like vine." "What's that?" Buzz said. "Vine," repeated the man. Someone shouted, "He wants wine, Buzz." Buzz, looking very disgusted, said, "We don't serve wine here." The foreigner replied, "Pleez, vee vant...zen, uh, fo bee-uh." Buzz growled, "I ain't got the slightest idea what you're talking about. And even if I did, I'm sure we ain't got it. We don't carry foreign food." The foreigner, trying to make himself understood, repeated, "Bee-uh, Bee-uh." All the regular customers were staring. "He wants a beer," shouted one of the men standing next to the television set. "Beer!" said Buzz; "why didn't you say so in the first place? How many beers do you want?" "Fo bee-uh, pleez," said the man. "What?" said Buzz. The man answered, "Fo. Von, two, zree, fo." Buzz grumbled, "Did you ever...," and went to get the drinks. The other customers just laughed.

When Buzz returned, the foreigners, sensing that they weren't welcome, drank their beers quickly and left. As soon as they were gone, Buzz said, "Did you ever…? I don't believe it! They couldn't even speak English!" The regular customers of the Home Town cafe laughed and laughed and laughed. In fact, they laughed for months. Someone would say, "Ve vud, pleez, like bee-uh"; then another would take up the cruel joke and say, "I vill sit here and drink zis drink." Then everyone would laugh wildly.

But the line that always got the biggest laugh came when someone stepped up to the counter and said, "Zen, uh, fo bee-uh."

So, when people hate or fear foreigners or strangers, like the "Home Town" customers, who mockingly said, "Zen, uh, fo bee-uh," we call such hatred or fear

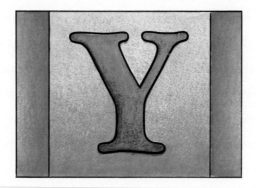

The vegetables in Farmer Finchley's field had always lived quiet lives. Planted in orderly fashion, each vegetable had its own row: the carrots were in one, the radishes in a second, the lettuce in a third, and the tomatoes in a fourth. Day after day, each vegetable knew what to expect of the next, because they all did the same thing: they went about the peaceful business of growing.

Life changed very little. The modest tomatoes always blushed prettily in the sun, and the aspiring, eager pole beans tried to climb higher and higher. The lazy watermelons lay in the sun and grew fatter and fatter. And the shy radishes hid their heads in the dirt.

Except for an occasional rainshower or windstorm, it was a quiet garden. There was almost no idle chatter, or giggling, or gossiping, or complaining. Oh, every now and then, the peas might say to the peppers, "Lovely weather we're having, isn't it?" And the peppers would shade their faces, look up at the cloudless sky, and answer, "Wonderful growing weather. Just look at the watermelons." Then they would both giggle,

92

knowing that watermelons were growing very fat. The carrots, of course, loved to wave their feathery tops in the wind and to compliment one another on the length of their hair. Perhaps once a week, the zucchinis would burst into song, singing "O, Sole Mio." But that was to be expected; and, anyway, the zucchinis had such lovely voices. Everything went along smoothly—until Farmer Finchley introduced a new plant in the field: yams.

Then everything changed. From the first green sprout, the yams never stopped talking—at the top of their voices. From dawn to dusk, they could be heard from one end of the garden to the other grumbling and complaining. "Look at that skinny bean pole," one of the yams would say; and the rest of the yams would snicker. "Why doesn't that carrot get a haircut? His feathery top is down to his shoulders," another yam would say; and all the yams would stare at the poor carrot, and point disapprovingly. Still another yam, a particularly impolite one, would say, "Do you see those watermelons? They're so fat they can't roll over." From morning till night, it was always the same thing: the yams never stopped talking and grumbling about the other vegetables in the garden.

From March to May, through June and July, there was no peace in Farmer Finchley's field. The yams talked and talked and talked. The other vegetables thought the yams would never be picked. Every day they prayed for the harvest and, in order to avoid the yams, grew as far away from them as possible. The beans climbed ever higher; the carrots leaned far to one side; and the radishes buried themselves deeper in the earth. Just when all the vegetables agreed that they would rather live with frost and hailstones and drought than with the constant chatter of yams, Farmer Finchley planted more. "Not another row of yams!" the other vegetables cried. "We can't stand their ceaseless complaints. We can't stand to hear one yam more!"

So, whenever you hear loud, non-stop talking, ceaseless complaining and chattering, think of the vegetables who said they couldn't stand to hear one yam more, and you will remember the word

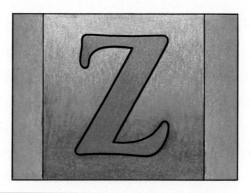

Henry Hawker was a medicine man. In a covered wagon he traveled through the wild west, from Washington to Wyoming, selling "Henry Hawker's Honest Herbal Syrup." Whenever he rode into a new town, he would park his wagon in front of the general store, roll back the canvas top, and announce:

> There's no better cure,
> You may be sure,
> For cold or hiccup
> Than this here syrup.

Holding a bottle in each hand, he would call to the people in the streets and invite them to try a sip of his magical medicine.

"Nothing like it in the whole wide world!" Henry would shout. "This here syrup will cure almost anything: sore throats, colds, dizziness, baldness, fatness, headaches, backaches, stomach aches, hangnails, calluses, fractures, and snakebite." But the same thing always happened. The people in the streets would walk right past his wagon without stopping.

Henry couldn't understand why no one listened. He was totally and utterly convinced that his syrup was the best in the world. "It must be the way I speak," thought Henry. "If only I could make a better speech, people would stop and buy my syrup." So Henry ordered a joke book from Chicago—a book about how to sell your product by making your customers laugh. After studying for several weeks, Henry was ready to try out what he had learned. He pulled into the Arizona town of "Somber" and reined his horses to a stop in front of the local church. Standing on the end of his wagon, he called to all the people on their way to Sunday services. "Ladies and Gentlemen! I have come before you to stand behind you to tell you a great event. This Wednesday is Saturday, and there'll be a mothers' meeting for fathers only. So bring your seats and sit on the floor—while I tell you about a 10¢ syrup that costs 20¢!" No one laughed and worse: no one stopped.

Henry was very upset. He believed his syrup was the best in the world. Why wouldn't anyone buy it? "I must have sent for the wrong book," he thought. So this time he ordered a book from Boston—a book about how to sell your product by making your customers cry. After studying for several weeks, Henry was ready to try out what he had learned. He pulled into the Colorado town of "No Tears" and reined his horses to a stop in front of the local saloon. Standing on the seat of his wagon, he cleared his throat and began. "Gentlemen!" he cried. The men in the saloon slowly filed outside. "My cupboard is bare. My dog has no bone. My cow is too weak to jump over the moon. I must sell my Honest Herbal syrup if I am ever again to sing a song of sixpence or have a pocketful of rye." No one cried and worse: no one cared. The men turned and started back into the saloon. "Half-price!" shouted Henry. In a moment the street was deserted.

Henry was heartbroken. He really did believe that in all the world there was no better medicine than his. So he devoted his life to the syrup, though he never sold a bottle. When he died, he was buried with the syrup in his hand; and on his tombstone was written just what Henry would have wished: "Here lies Henry Hawker, and here too lies his Honest Herbal Syrup. He believed in it, and that is why he tried to sell it."

So, whenever a person believes that his product (or idea) is the best in the world, remember Henry Hawker who believed in his Honest Herbal Syrup, although he could not sell it, and you will remember the word

Zealot